SAVING YOUR CHURCH FROM ITSELF

SIX SUBTLE BEHAVIORS THAT TEAR TEAMS APART AND HOW TO STOP THEM

STUDY GUIDE

Cover design: Sara Young
Cover photo: Brenton Stanley

ISBN: 978-1-960678-43-0   1 2 3 4 5 6 7 8 9 10

Printed in the United States of America

CHRIS SONKSEN

SAVING YOUR CHURCH FROM ITSELF

SIX SUBTLE BEHAVIORS THAT TEAR TEAMS APART AND HOW TO STOP THEM

STUDY GUIDE

ARROWS &
STONES

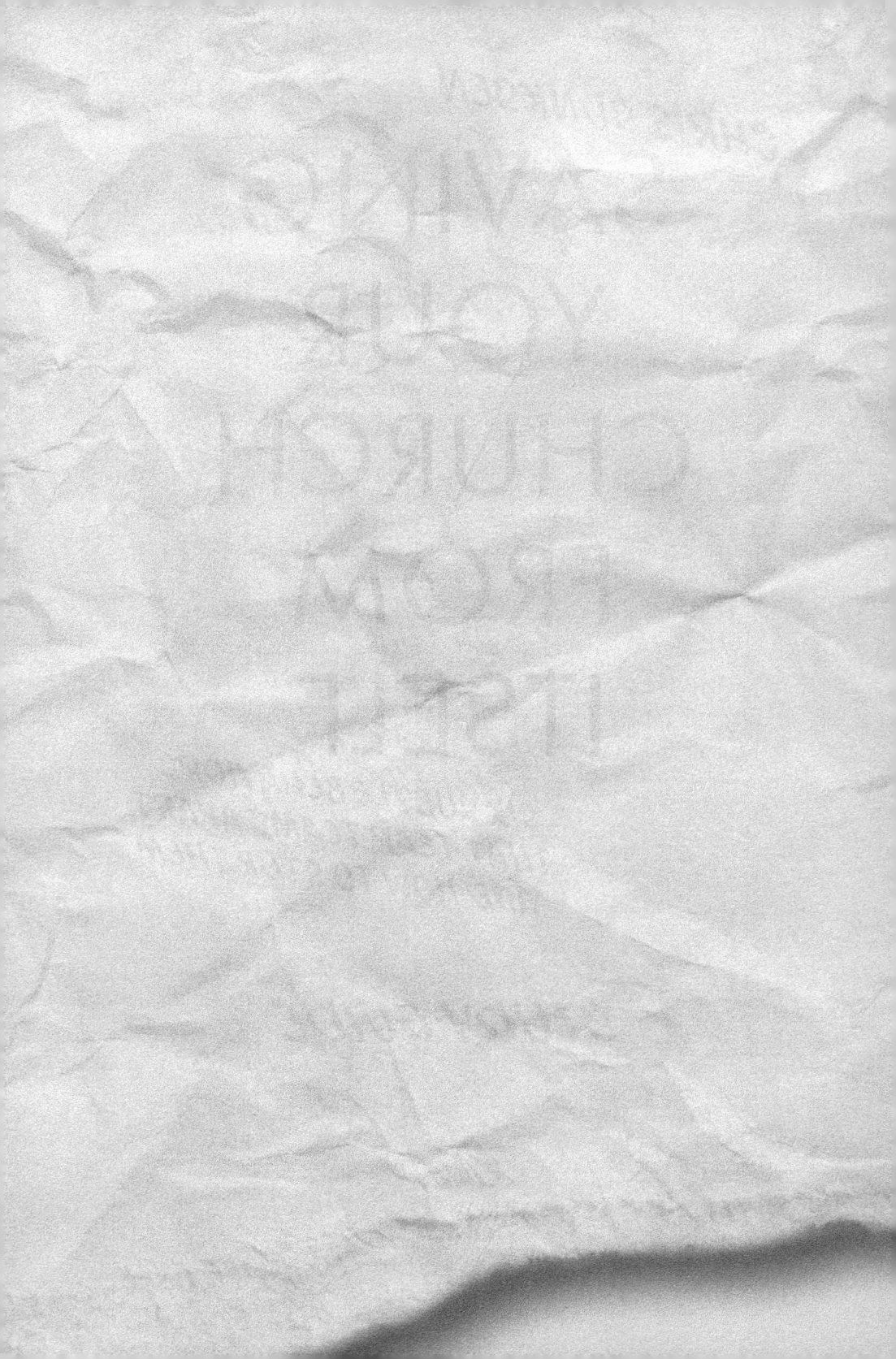

CONTENTS

THE ENEMY'S GREATEST STRATEGY— LEADERDRIFT

When the enemy takes a run at your church,
he won't do it through those who attend it;
he will do it through those that lead it.

READING TIME

As you read Chapter 1: "The Enemy's Greatest Strategy—Leaderdrift" in *Saving Your Church from Itself*, review, reflect on, and respond to the text by answering the following questions.

REFLECT AND TAKE ACTION:

In your own words, what is leaderdrift?

_____

_____

_____

_____

_____

_____

_____

Have you ever experienced leaderdrift?
Explain the situation.

_____

_____

_____

_____

_____

_____

_____

Why do you think the enemy uses leaderdrift
to attack churches?

_____

_____

_____

_____

_____

_____

> *It is not an enemy who taunts me—I could bear that.*
> *It is not my foes who so arrogantly insult me—I could*
> *have hidden from them. Instead, it is you—my equal, my*
> *companion and close friend. What good fellowship we*
> *once enjoyed as we walked together to the house of God.*
>
> **—Psalm 55:12-14 (NLT)**

Consider the scripture above and answer the following questions:

What stands out to you from these verses?

_____

_____

_____

_____

_____

_____

How can you relate to David?

_____

_____

_____

_____

_____

_____

How can you defend against leaderdrift?

_____

_____

_____

_____

_____

_____

_____

What are some of the different types of drift? Have you ever seen these in yourself or other leaders?

_____

_____

_____

_____

_____

_____

What are the negative effects of leaderdrift? Are any of these present in your church or mindset?

_____

_____

_____

_____

_____

_____

Why do you think so many leaders attempt to rationalize leaderdrift?

_____

_____

_____

_____

_____

_____

CHAPTER 2

TEAM ALIGNMENT ISN'T A GOOD THING— IT'S EVERYTHING

Alignment won't secure success, but misalignment will secure failure.

READING TIME

As you read Chapter 2: "Team Alignment Isn't a Good Thing—It's Everything" in *Saving Your Church from Itself*, review, reflect on, and respond to the text by answering the following questions.

REFLECT AND TAKE ACTION:

What is team alignment? On a scale from 1-10 (with 1 being low and 10 being high) how would you rate your current alignment?

1   2   3   4   5   6   7   8   9   10

_____

_____

_____

_____

_____

_____

_____

_____

_____

What are the dangers that come with misalignment?

_____

_____

_____

_____

_____

_____

_____

_____

_____

_____

_____

_____

Have you ever been a part of a team that was misaligned? What was the result? Was it fixed?

_____

_____

_____

_____

_____

_____

Are distance and disrespect present in your organization? Explain.

_____

_____

_____

_____

_____

_____

Why do you think criticism and misalignment go hand in hand? In what forms does this criticism manifest?

_____

_____

_____

_____

_____

_____

_____

What are a few of the benefits of team alignment? Is your team experiencing all these benefits?

_____

_____

_____

_____

_____

_____

_____

Are you a confident leader? How do you think an aligned team helps a leader's confidence levels?

_____

_____

_____

_____

_____

_____

_____

_____

DRIFTING TOWARD PRIDE

Pride can consume who we are and turn us into a version of ourselves that we once said we would never become.

READING TIME

As you read Chapter 3: "Drifting Toward Pride" in *Saving Your Church from Itself*, review, reflect on, and respond to the text by answering the following questions.

Define pride. What would pride look like in your leadership role?

_____

_____

_____

_____

_____

_____

_____

What does pride keep us from? Has your personal pride ever kept you from anything on the list provided?

_____

_____

_____

_____

_____

_____

What does pride cause? Which of these effects have you seen or experienced?

_____

_____

_____

_____

_____

_____

_____

> *God blesses those who are poor and realize their*
> *need for him, for the Kingdom of Heaven is theirs.*
>
> **—Matthew 5:3 (NLT)**

Consider the scripture above and answer the following questions:

What do you feel is the meaning of this verse?

_____

_____

_____

_____

_____

_____

_____

What kind of "poor" do you think Jesus is speaking of in this passage?

_____

_____

_____

_____

_____

_____

What stands out to you from the prideful campus pastor story told in this chapter? Where do you think things went wrong?

_____

_____

_____

_____

_____

_____

_____

_____

Which of the early signs of drifting toward pride have you seen in your own ministry or someone else's? How did you respond?

_____

_____

_____

_____

_____

_____

_____

_____

_____

How do you defend against pride taking control? How can you do a better job in this area?

_____

_____

_____

_____

_____

_____

_____

_____

DRIFTING TOWARD ARTIFICIAL HARMONY

Avoiding the difficult and awkward
conversations won't bring harmony.

READING TIME

As you read Chapter 4: "Drifting Toward Artificial Harmony" in *Saving Your Church from Itself*, review, reflect on, and respond to the text by answering the following questions.

What is artificial harmony?

_____

_____

_____

_____

_____

_____

_____

_____

_____

_____

_____

Why is artificial harmony so dangerous to an organization?

_____

_____

_____

_____

_____

_____

_____

_____

_____

_____

> *If a kingdom is divided against itself,*
> *that kingdom cannot stand.*
>
> **—Mark 3:24 (NIV)**

Consider the scripture above and answer the following questions:

What does a kingdom divided against itself look like?

_____

_____

_____

_____

_____

How does being divided prevent a kingdom from standing?

_____

_____

_____

_____

_____

Which of the four signs of artificial harmony have you experienced at some point in your lifetime? Were these the result of a false harmony among your team?

_____

_____

_____

_____

_____

_____

Are any of the four signs of artificial harmony present in your organization now?

_____

_____

_____

_____

_____

Have you ever neglected or put off confronting something you knew was an issue in your organization? What was it? What was the end result?

_____

_____

_____

_____

_____

What is the difference between signs two and three—distance and disconnection?

_____

_____

_____

_____

_____

In your own words, how does artificial harmony lead to dishonor? How is this dishonor shown?

_____

_____

_____

_____

DRIFTING TOWARD ISOLATION: WHEN THE CALLING TURNS INTO A CAREER

That's what isolation does—it opens the door to distorted perceptions and negative assumptions. It exaggerates our feelings and turns them into false facts.

READING
TIME

As you read
Chapter 5:
"Drifting
Toward
Isolation:
When the
Calling Turns
into a Career"
in *Saving Your
Church from
Itself*, review,
reflect on,
and respond
to the text by
answering
the following
questions.

REFLECT AND TAKE ACTION:

Have you ever experienced isolation?
Describe the experience. Did you realize you
were isolated? How did you feel?

_____

_____

_____

_____

_____

_____

_____

What is the big danger we face when we
become isolated from others?

_____

_____

_____

_____

_____

_____

Do you think the older brother in the parable
of the prodigal son was justified in his anger
toward his father? Why or why not?

_____

_____

_____

_____

_____

_____

Is there anyone on your team who might feel underappreciated or unseen? How can you change this?

_____

_____

_____

_____

_____

_____

_____

_____

_____

> *"Holy Father, protect them by Your name, the name You gave Me, so that they may be one as We are one."*
>
> **—John 17:11 (NIV)**

Consider the scripture above and answer the following questions:

Why did Jesus feel the need to pray for His disciples?

_____

_____

_____

_____

_____

_____

_____

_____

What strength would our organizations find if we were one as the Father, Son, and Holy Spirit are one?

_____

_____

_____

_____

_____

_____

Have you ever seen any of the three early signs of isolation drift? Which? Are any of these signs present in your team members?

_____

_____

_____

_____

_____

_____

_____

As the leader, what can you do to better unify your team and make sure that no one feels isolated?

_____

_____

_____

_____

_____

_____

DRIFTING TOWARD A CRITICAL SPIRIT: FROM CRITIQUING TO CRITICIZING

There is always an underlying cause that shifts a person away from being constructive and into being destructive.

READING TIME

As you read Chapter 6: "Drifting Toward a Critical Spirit: From Critiquing to Criticizing" in *Saving Your Church from Itself*, review, reflect on, and respond to the text by answering the following questions.

REFLECT AND TAKE ACTION:

In your own words, define what a critical spirit is and why it is detrimental to your church.

_____

_____

_____

_____

_____

_____

_____

What is the difference between critiquing and criticizing?

_____

_____

_____

_____

_____

_____

_____

What are the reasons for people falling into a critical spirit?

_____

_____

_____

_____

_____

_____

What are the nine things that can lead to a critical spirit?

_____

_____

_____

_____

_____

_____

Of the nine things you listed, which do you most need to work on?

_____

_____

_____

_____

_____

_____

How can you defend and free yourself from a critical spirit?

_____

_____

_____

_____

_____

_____

Have you ever participated in a negativity fast? What's stopping you from trying one tomorrow or the next week?

_____

_____

_____

_____

_____

_____

Who do you have in your life who is a good influence and can hold you accountable?

_____

_____

_____

_____

_____

_____

What amends might you need to make before you move forward?

_____

_____

_____

_____

_____

_____

DRIFTING TOWARD DIVISION: MORE THAN ONE VISION ALWAYS CREATES DIVISION

If you see someone on your team drifting toward division, you must have the courage to call it out.

READING TIME

As you read Chapter 7: "Drifting Toward Division: More Than One Vision Always Creates Division" in *Saving Your Church from Itself*, review, reflect on, and respond to the text by answering the following questions.

REFLECT AND TAKE ACTION:

Has your church ever experienced internal division? How did it feel? What was the result?

_____
_____
_____
_____
_____
_____
_____

What is a "sheep-like" leader? Do you possess any of the characteristics of this type of leader? How can you tell?

_____
_____
_____
_____
_____
_____
_____

What is a "wolf-like" leader? Do you possess any of these qualities? How do you know?

_____
_____
_____
_____
_____
_____

How does division take root?

_____

_____

_____

_____

_____

_____

_____

_____

What are the warning signs of a divisive spirit? Do you see any of these signs present in your team? If you did, what would you do?

_____

_____

_____

_____

_____

_____

_____

_____

What are some practical steps you can take to defend against division?

_____

_____

_____

_____

_____

_____

_____

_____

_____

_____

Is it possible to mend division after the fact? If so, how?

_____

_____

_____

_____

_____

_____

_____

_____

_____

_____

_____

DRIFTING TOWARD A GRADUAL SHUTDOWN

Your responsibility is to be aware of the triggers that could lead to a shutdown.

READING TIME

As you read Chapter 8: "Drifting Toward a Gradual Shutdown" in *Saving Your Church from Itself*, review, reflect on, and respond to the text by answering the following questions.

REFLECT AND TAKE ACTION:

How would you define a gradual shutdown in your own words?

_____

_____

_____

_____

_____

_____

_____

_____

_____

_____

_____

Have you ever seen one of your team succumb to a gradual shutdown? Briefly describe the situation.

_____

_____

_____

_____

_____

_____

_____

_____

_____

_____

What are the seven situations that can trigger a gradual shutdown?

_____

_____

_____

_____

_____

_____

_____

_____

_____

_____

Of these seven triggers, which do you feel your team is most in danger of?

_____

_____

_____

_____

_____

_____

_____

_____

_____

_____

Once someone has "shutdown," are they permanently lost? Why or why not?

_____

_____

_____

_____

_____

_____

_____

_____

_____

_____

Have you ever failed to meet expectations that your team was counting on you to meet? How have you cleared the air after the fact?

_____

_____

_____

_____

_____

_____

_____

_____

_____

_____

IF YOU'RE THE LEADER AND YOU SEE IT

Your delay will only increase the cost your ministry and leadership will have to pay.

READING TIME

As you read Chapter 9: "If You're the Leader and You See It" in *Saving Your Church from Itself*, review, reflect on, and respond to the text by answering the following questions.

As the leader, what warning signs do you see? How long have you known about them?

_____

_____

_____

_____

_____

_____

_____

What is the danger of ignoring or not acting on warning signs?

_____

_____

_____

_____

_____

_____

What is stopping you from confronting these issues? Fear of not being liked? The fear of fallout?

_____

_____

_____

_____

_____

_____

If you do nothing about the warning signs and let the situation continue on as is, what do you think will be the result?

_____

_____

_____

_____

_____

_____

_____

_____

Have you ever been guilty of approaching a problem in one of the incorrect ways listed in this chapter? What was the result? What did you learn?

_____

_____

_____

_____

_____

_____

_____

_____

Which of the constructive approaches to difficult conversations do you need to do a better job of when confronting issues? List and explain all that apply.

_____

_____

_____

_____

_____

_____

_____

_____

_____

_____

Are you willing to fight for your team's health and alignment? What might that entail?

_____

_____

_____

_____

_____

_____

_____

_____

_____

_____

IF YOU'RE THE TEAM MEMBER AND YOU FEEL IT

*Let's be the kind of leaders who choose to
do right, even when we feel the tension.*

REFLECT AND TAKE ACTION:

READING TIME

As you read Chapter 10: "If You're the Team Member and You Feel It" in *Saving Your Church from Itself*, review, reflect on, and respond to the text by answering the following questions.

Have you ever felt one of your leaders drifting? How did it make you feel? How did you respond?

_____

_____

_____

_____

_____

_____

What is leadership tension? Is this normal? Is it good? How does one manage leadership tension?

_____

_____

_____

_____

_____

_____

What are the symptoms of improperly managed leadership tension? Which of these symptoms have you experienced?

_____

_____

_____

_____

_____

_____

What is personal tension? How can personal tension get in the way of leadership?

_____

_____

_____

_____

_____

_____

In which of the three common ways listed in this chapter have you responded when confronted about your personal tension? Why did you respond this way?

_____

_____

_____

_____

_____

_____

_____

Of the ten desired traits every lead pastor wants their team to possess, which do you feel your team excels at?

_____

_____

_____

_____

_____

_____

_____

Which of the ten traits do you think your team collectively needs to work on?

_____

_____

_____

_____

_____

_____

What are some of the principles in this book that you can begin striving for immediately in your church?

_____

_____

_____

_____

_____

_____

www.ingramcontent.com/pod-product-compliance
Lightning Source LLC
Chambersburg PA
CBHW070051100426
42734CB00040B/2981